HOT BUTTON MOTIVATION

*Increase Sales, Improve Relationships,
and Understand Why People Act and React!*

MICHELLE GLOVER

authorHOUSE®

AuthorHouse™
1663 Liberty Drive
Bloomington, IN 47403
www.authorhouse.com
Phone: 1-800-839-8640

First published by AuthorHouse 3/24/2011

ISBN: 978-1-4567-5678-9 (e)
ISBN: 978-1-4567-5679-6 (dj)
ISBN: 978-1-4567-5680-2 (sc)

Library of Congress Control Number: 2011904467

Printed in the United States of America

Cover design concept by Bryon Lehl

My car was in the shop so I picked the girls up in a beautiful red Tundra loaner truck. It was a real treat for my middle school kids who were used to the conservative navy blue mini-van. The pleading started almost immediately, "Pleeaassee can we buy this car?" "Please Mom, this is SO cool!"

Suddenly, Coleen interrupted the melee. "Wait, she won't listen to this. She is a Love Hot Button." Several minutes of whispering followed. And then this pitch:

Cassie: "Mom, a lot of our friends are moving, you could really help them if you had this truck."

Courtney: "Yeah, Ma, and your people at work always have signs and stuff."

Coleen: "Mom this truck would help everyone."

I couldn't believe it – they were doing a better job selling this vehicle than the guy at the car lot!

Oh boy, I thought, maybe I shouldn't be bringing my work home with me! But my second thought was how great is it that such young girls understood how to get their point across and motivate me.

To Cynthia

Thank you for understanding and encouraging my obsession. Your support, ideas and observations have made the journey intriguing and fun. I love you.

TABLE OF CONTENTS

INTRODUCTION

The moment I realized the power of Hot Buttons I was not on the sales floor. I was working for a large national builder as a Performance Coach and assigned my team the task of discovering Hot Buttons with strangers. My family agreed to indulge my whim and play along. Our first opportunity presented itself at dinner. We gathered at a local restaurant that was relatively quiet and gave us time to question our waitress; but boy was she tough! We tried everything to get her to open up. "Do you like working here?", "How old are your kids?", and "Is it safe to leave so late?" These are typically questions that naturally open people up and give insight into how they think. We kept questioning to no avail. Finally my mom hit pay dirt with the question:

"My sister is coming to town. Do you have suggestions for what we should do?" BAM!!

The waitress quickly put her tray on an empty table, kneeled next to my mom and started running through activities we should explore. I couldn't believe it; Diana, our waitress, went from surly to animated in seconds! Recreation! That was her Hot Button. We were positively stunned and it left us wanting more. We watched and played with discovery wherever we went. Hot Buttons became our language and the way our family described people and situations. I was now prepared to circle back and play with the knowledge on the sales floor which is where I was introduced to these concepts in the first place.

Because several national home builders incorporate Hot Buttons into their training materials, I was exposed to the material in a variety of ways. Most of them involved telling sales agents to memorize twelve motivators because university research shows that all purchasing decisions can be categorized in this way. Agents are given brief descriptions about emotional ties that Hot Button categories represent and told to look for "signs" in order to work features into sales presentations. For instance, questions about money may signal a Finance Hot Button triggering discussion on energy efficiency and the savings in utilities costs. Revelations about children should prompt the agent to showcase the family room with the assumption that he/she is working with a Family Hot Button. I was fascinated with the concept but felt it was too superficial. I wanted to know the whole story.

A personal quest to understand the psychological drivers helped me with a new understanding of the sales process. I teamed up with brilliant agents who shared my fascination. We gathered more information, tried new approaches and had so much fun! We learned to turn guarded, scared prospects into really happy homeowners. Everywhere I worked the sales numbers AND our customer satisfaction scores improved dramatically with the use of these concepts. Once we really understood who we were meeting, our transactions became more fulfilling for everyone involved.

Although Hot Button concepts were discovered as part of a research project about buying decisions, this book is not just for salespeople. Once you understand the relationship of Hot Button motivators to all interactions you will be able to apply the concepts to relationships at home, work and with friends. A great deal of my career has been spent in new home sales, so I draw several examples from real estate. But as the waitress example illustrates, understanding and using Hot Button information will open communication no matter what type of sales or personal situation you encounter.

Why am I compelled to write this book? The time is right. Sales are brutal in every industry. Communication, in general, is moving more toward digital technology and away from personal contact. It feels like we are forgetting that people are individuals and live by their own internal guide. Technology and media have changed our world and people struggle to adjust. Companies, campuses, and individuals have asked me to present these concepts so that they might be able to develop their communication skills. My hope is that this book serves as a resource for individuals to improve their lives by enriching communication and thus their relationships. I am, after all, a Love Hot Button and want everyone to be happy!

I've also been asked over the years how I know this information is accurate. The Hot Button research was done so long ago that it isn't conveniently stored on a flash drive somewhere. Years ago I attempted to retrieve the information from the university that sponsored the study but they were unable to locate the original research. Other than builders' materials that have been reprinting Hot Button information for over a decade (sometimes incorrectly or with new spins), there is nothing else I can find. I have, however, built relationships with thousands of customers, managed hundreds of agents, and worked in a variety of business situations. In short, I offer my own experiential evidence to support my theories. The salespeople I train appreciate that I have tested this hypothesis in every area of life and found the results to be consistent. Once you've read my book, try playing with the concepts yourself. The truth and reward are in the improved communications.

To visualize Hot Button concepts, pick a couple of people you know really well like a spouse, child or sibling. Use the information to identify which category they would fall into. Think, for example, about what car they drive, how they spend money, their language, and where they spend their time. Why do they make these decisions? The following chapters will help you put the pieces together.

OVERVIEW

A university study determined there are twelve factors that psychologically drive people. The psychological drivers are labeled as Hot Buttons. Each of us falls into one of the following categories:

Recreation	Investment
Love	Ego
Security	Sex
Culture	Convenience
Family	Finance
Prestige	Privacy

Most people have difficulty pinpointing which driver applies to them and when pressed, may claim that they are a combination.

My first experience with this confusion unfolded at a sales meeting. I asked 30 agents to categorize themselves. I was shocked to discover that the majority of the salespeople identified themselves as Finance. The exercise left me really confused. Does the sales profession attract a particular Hot Button? Maybe, but I doubted it. I knew my agents; their paychecks were important yet money wasn't what they talked about all day. They loved their families, bragged about grandchildren, obsessed about sports, and exchanged wine tasting tips (yes, we live in California) . . . So what did I miss?

I was missing the reason WHY they wanted the big paychecks. What I should have initially asked them was: "What will you use the money for?" After all, these are purchasing *motives*, right? I learned a valuable lesson that day, and discovered another key to training salespeople. Make them dig deep and question themselves, question their buyers, and question anyone else they need to understand.

In more recent years I have been challenged about the possibility of having multiple Hot Buttons. Some of the confusion arises because priorities can overlap between Hot Buttons. My opinion is that our core motivator ultimately boils down to one. While writing this book, my editor identified herself as a Security Hot Button, but I thought she might really be Family. So I posed this simple question:

"If your sister needed something and it would undermine your security, would you do it?"

Her response was immediate, "I would take a bullet for her." She picked her sister without any concern for herself; a Security Hot Button would ask what the threat is or make other qualifying remarks. I would say the immediate and emphatic response revealed her true nature to be Family.

In everyone's life there comes a time when a difficult decision needs to be made. If, while reading my book, you start to wrestle with your identity, narrow it to two. Like the example above, ask yourself what you would do if a situation put the two Hot Buttons at odds. Most people have no problem deciding what their priority would be.

Another tactic might be to keep asking WHY until you find that it all boils down to one. Take, for instance, a Love Hot Button who thinks she overlaps with Convenience. After answering "why" a few times, she finds that the reason she seeks to make things easy is to avoid chaos and misunderstandings for all.

Discovering core drivers takes patience and listening skills. Identifying the correct category is fun and rewarding. Getting co-workers, buyers and everyone else around you to listen is invaluable!

BRIEF DESCRIPTIONS

Take a moment to identify your own psychological driver. Below is a brief summary description of each Hot Button. The following chapters will explain in greater detail and give examples.

Ego – All about them, doesn't care what anyone thinks, may show blatant disrespect to others

Prestige – It's all about keeping up with the Jones'; will go to any length to seem successful and get people to like them

Finance – Short term money concerns - all they can think about is how to keep the lights on

Investment – Long term financial, personal, and spiritual gain - will sacrifice short term comfort for long term gain

Culture – Will make decisions causing discomfort to everyone including their own family to meet cultural guidelines

Family – Wants nothing more than the picket fence and home sweet home even if upsets friends/work/others

Love – Wants everyone to be happy, looks for win-win long after others give up

Privacy – Sometimes looks like security but is often just conservative upbringing. Has plenty of connections just doesn't share feelings or personal life easily.

Security – Need to feel feet firmly planted financially, physically and emotionally.

Recreation – All about fun – Lots of toys (boats, golf, ski…) - But the fun doesn't need to be instant; they will camp and participate in other activities that require effort. Will sacrifice better job and sometimes family for less stress/more personal and a more "fun" lifestyle

Sex – Instant gratification – It's a beer commercial. They want everything to be easy and fun.

Convenience – Goes to great lengths to set up procedures that make things easier. This is difficult to determine because they can be confused with others who are saving time to accomplish something else like family time or praise at work.

HOT BUTTON
DESCRIPTIONS

CONVENIENCE

Most people save time so they focus on achieving personal goals; they want more time with family, improve financial gain, etc. . . But there is a group of people who are merely on a quest for easy. If you see someone circling the parking lot to find the closest spot and then they jump right into conversation without any of the typical preamble– you found your convenience person!

I recently had an opportunity to work with the staff at a local college. One of the counselors insisted he was a Convenience Hot Button so we dug a little deeper and here is the description he gave of himself:

"I want everything to be easy. The first thing I do at a new job is see how I can improve the system. Until I met my wife I never really dated, but she made it easy to stay in the relationship. When it comes to video games I will give up and never touch it again unless I am good at it immediately. Even sports, I only played the ones that came naturally."

What is amazing is that he is a very accomplished professional with a Masters Degree and a happy home life. Even though he has an internal need for life to be easy – he is certainly not lazy. This is a very important distinction with the Convenience group.

It is common for engineers and others of similar professions to be preoccupied with efficiency. They see waste of any kind as stupidity. In general, Convenience people want all processes simplified. If you want to help, ask what they want to achieve and stick to the program. To avoid frustration on their part, simplify complicated processes and hold any information until asked.

The need for such succinct interactions can make it hard for this Hot Button to socialize. If you know someone like this, find a topic they love and jump right in. Let them spend time in their comfort zone! In sales, they want a summary page for your product and want you to skip presentations.

SUMMARY:

Wants: *Logical, simple solutions. Saving time &
energy is main priority.*

Avoid: *Talking too much, complicated products,
forms or processes.*

CULTURE

Do visions of diversity posters clutter your mind when you read the word culture? That's a typical reaction but really, Culture is more subtle.

I have a personal example. As I was learning about Hot Buttons, I made a conscious effort to watch the people around me. The most confusing subject was my Mom. Although I was leaning toward a Family Hot Button, it didn't explain some things like shooing us all out of the family room when the Boston Red Sox were playing, or refusing to eat foods she really enjoyed because "she didn't grow up with it". Then I witnessed a conversation with a stranger who recognized my mom's Boston accent (it IS wicked cool). The glint in her eye was obvious and it explained everything to me. Her Hot Button is Culture. She is a Bostonian through and through. Her gauge of what is right or wrong comes from that upbringing. She continues to reinforce it by conferring with her sisters & brothers and watching Boston news & sports. I love it. It has given our family a rich, proud history to build the foundation of our own lives. And if we need a decision from her – well – we just need to make sure to measure up to her Bostonian view of the world!

We will often pick up on glaring cultural clues. Numbers, placement of a door, and an inability to do business on a particular day are all fairly obvious signs that there are cultural considerations at work. But more subtle cultural clues hold the key to a more difficult customer. Ask questions until you see the sparkle in their eye. You may discover a place they lived, a religion, or a group to which they relate. If you struggle to define a Culture Hot Button, look for clues like accents, jewelry (Claddagh rings, Buddha, Cross, etc . . .) or anything that might spark a conversation. If someone is a Culture Hot Button, asking is the best way to put the pieces together.

Verbally the clues are in comments like "In our family we wouldn't" or "Where I grew up". When a person is so proud of their culture that they define themselves by it, they light up and become animated. The enthusiastic spirit signals Culture.

Wants: To honor their heritage or those with whom they identify. Want others to acknowledge and understand that these groups are important to them.

Avoid: Brushing over those comments or minimizing their beliefs.

EGO & PRESTIGE

Ego: an exaggerated sense of self-importance and a feeling of superiority to other people

Prestige: honor, awe, or high opinion inspired by or derived from a high-ranking, influential, or successful person or product

The terms seem interchangeable in our society, don't they? People have trouble distinguishing these two from each other, but as you can see from the definitions, they are virtually opposites. Ego is completely self-involved while the Prestige is a position derived from an external force.

Often training materials blur the lines between Ego and Prestige, but the reality is that they behave very differently. An Ego person couldn't care less what people think and may go out of their way to make people cringe. Prestige Hot

Buttons do ONLY what is socially acceptable. The following descriptions should help you distinguish:

Have you ever met someone who just doesn't care about their appearance? A person who uses the words "I" and "Me" in every sentence? This is the quintessential Ego Hot Button. They are typically in professions that allow them complete control (entrepreneurs, professors, sales, other professions that allow supervisory power without moving up in the traditional way).

My favorite story about an Ego Hot Button took place during a training session with about 25 agents. I was describing some of the telltale signs of an Ego personality: "If you see a middle-aged, overweight man jammed into a tiny sports car – probably a convertible – he is an ego Hot Button. The Prestige Hot Button would never allow themselves to look so ridiculous squeezing in and out the car."

Immediately a hand went up. Naively I responded, "Yes, question?" He said "No, I AM that guy."! I was *so* embarrassed but remarkably HE wasn't! Why? He doesn't care what people think. The car, as well as everything else in his life, is for HIS enjoyment. Even admitting that in front of a room of his peers doesn't matter.

Because "Egos" don't care about others, they will often seem rude or inconsiderate. Some salespeople are offended and miss out on an easy sale because a prospect acts abrasively. The only way to make progress with the Ego Hot Button is to agree and make sure their every opinion is heard. Make them feel like royalty and anything you want is yours!

Prestige Hot Buttons, on the other hand, are eager to look happy and won't tell you if you are on the wrong track for fear of appearing confrontational. They want to know that they are thought of highly. People with Prestige Hot Buttons dress in the most current fashions, drive an expensive car, and want to know that they have something to brag about when any transaction is complete. Not to satisfy an ego, but so they can bring it up at work, parties, and soccer games.

The best way to relate to a Prestige Hot Button is to make sure that everything appears to be picture perfect. Give them lots to be happy about and reasons to feel that people would envy them. (Posting a thank you to their Facebook wall goes a long way.) In sales, to assure success with a Prestige Hot Button, know your product. Discuss only the most popular features and why past buyers loved them. Do you have satisfaction stats? Telling 3rd party stories where everyone ended up happy is very effective. They want to know that they will be part of a large and happy crowd. And always have written information and pictures for them to show others; it will remind them of why they are so smitten with your product.

Prestige buyers are your best advertisement. If you make them happy, they will tell everyone!

SUMMARY:

Ego Wants: To make themselves happy. They don't need external validation, and feel others are there to assist in their happiness.

Avoid with Ego: Disagreeing about anything. Comparing to others.

Prestige Wants: To be admired. Needs validation that others think like them.

Avoid with Prestige: Embarrassing them in any way, or confrontation.

FAMILY

In traditional situations, Family Hot Buttons are the easiest to recognize. But contemporary families come in different varieties. "Family" can be siblings, in-laws, domestic partners and even close knit friends. My focus here is on conventional families because they are present in greater numbers. You may find yourself relating to Family even though the examples are traditional.

Let me start by stating, you do not have to be a Family Hot Button to be a good parent. There are beneficial family aspects to each Hot Button. The difference is that someone who is Family motivated does not want outside influences and are very willing to make sacrifices to stay within the bubble of their home life. The Family Hot Buttons will work 9-5:00 and not a minute later. No parties and living paycheck to paycheck is fine; they don't care what others think. . . Home is where the heart is.

There are Hot Buttons that appear very similar to Family. The Love Hot Button, for instance, will make an impression for their over the top pride in their family, but the key difference is in how they treat others. It's not that they are mean to others; they just see family as an exclusive group.

The best example is my coworker who identifies himself as a Love Hot Button. When I question him about his car, he admits it only has 4 seatbelts – one for each of his kids and his wife. He purchased it so his wife would have a safer ride and he picked mauve because it was close to his daughter's favorite color – pink. Still sounds like it could be Love, right? So how does this differ? Seatbelts – Family Hot Button only has as many belts as his immediate circle needs. A Love Hot Button wants as many as possible to fit friends, family, everyone!

While we are at it, how does this differ from Prestige? Color. What would the neighbors think about a pink car! What about Investment? Brand – it is so non-descript, I can't even remember the brand!

SUMMARY:

Wants: To care for and spend time with their family to the exclusion of all else.

Avoid: Taking time or resources from the family.

FINANCE

For many, periods of trying financial times force us to think about the impacts of every purchase, no matter how small. For example, the "Great Recession" has many worried about the monthly impact of basic expenses. Financial pressure forces people to make choices that inherently go against their very nature.

But how they justify expenses and prioritize budgets says a lot about their true nature. For example, unemployed parents across the nation continue to find the funds to pay for dance and karate classes for the kids. This probably signifies a Family Hot Button but it could be that parents don't want the neighbors to know how financially strapped they are (Prestige).

Exceptions are those who experienced financially challenging childhoods where the need to count pennies became ingrained in their psyche. These are true Finance Hot Buttons. Working with a large active adult community, I saw this first hand. Preparing for a disaster and being financially sound is a result of a Great Depression/Post-Depression Era upbringing. Being financially sound meant staying alive and together; such internal messaging stays ingrained. They are prepared to make people unhappy, and they aren't worried about their own preferences. The bottom line comes first, even when they are extremely financially stable.

Selling during an economic downturn can be stressful. The dilemma is whether or not to "convince" someone to buy when money is tight. Only you can make that call, but I offer this advice – ask yourself if they will kick themselves later. If your product meets a need that brings long term happiness, then push to get them to see the value. Most people are willing to endure short term "pain" if it meets their true Hot Button needs. For example, buying a home right now is a true stretch for employees forced to take pay cuts or workers who lost investment and savings over the last few years. But for these very same people, the need to entertain, invest, raise a family, etc . . . . doesn't disappear. It is incumbent on the real estate industry to help prospects see that short term brown bag lunches allow them to meet those bigger, more important needs.

How do you uncover intrinsic needs? The first way is a proven sales tactic called, "waving a magic wand". In other words, ask "if money were not a factor, what would you do?" Getting someone to visualize life without the financial struggles may help them see that the current situation is temporary and buying is a step to a better future.

Another way to discover a person's true nature is to find out what they would do with a large sum of money. Make sure the answer is spontaneous, and you will know what the priority is. Don't let them get away with "pay bills" – that can be the financial stress talking. The pure answer will be something like a trip, a new car, or shoes! Now you have discovered their authentic Hot Button!

Uncovering core priorities allow you to "re-adjust" the budget. Help Finance Hot Buttons eliminate less important items that might just leave room for your purchase!

Once you unveil what will make them happy long term, you can make the decision about whether this is just a tough sale or a future sale.

SUMMARY:

Wants: To make ends meet – needs to be able to justify spending every penny. In more "permanent" situations living frugally is ingrained, and has nothing to do with bank balance.

Avoid: Speaking in terms of just cost; it's painful. Get to the emotional reasons behind the immediate situation.

INVESTMENT

Commonly confused with Finance, The Investment Hot Button is actually the exact opposite. Investment Hot Buttons will stretch money in the short term so they can invest for long term gain. Like Finance, it is easy to think a preoccupation with money is a true psychological motivator. Remember to ask "WHY?" to clarify the intent. Some will appear to want a long term investment, but are actually hoping a successful investment will help meet another goal, like retirement or inheritance for their children.

Trying to understand why they are looking long term may hold the key to making a sale. Investment is, by nature, cold and impersonal. By bringing the personal aspect into the discussion, you are better able to understand the transaction and the buyer. There may be short term tradeoffs that satisfy the long term objective as well. As an example, if the long term goal is leaving something for the family, find a way to make the family happy *now* and in the future. Are you saving some money or time? Be sure to remind the customer that these benefits, too, are an investment in their family.

Investment doesn't need to be just about money. People who are truly investment-minded also invest in long marriages and relationships. They will also commit to one company for years and invest their energies into causes in which they believe.

In the end, the Investment Hot Button is all about sharing the vision of the future. If Investment Hot Buttons know you understand the goals and support them, they will be open to you.

SUMMARY:

Wants: To see growth in all aspects of their lives. Provide proof of any benefits if you want them to support.

Avoid: Talking about short term gain. Talking in generalities.

LOVE

"Can't we all just get along?" That's the motto of the Love Hot Button. They truly seek to make everyone happy because their own happiness depends on it. More than just people-pleasers, this personality goes beyond looking for a quick solution to avoid conflict. They may actually be confrontational to assure that the end result satisfies the majority of people.

The desire for harmony is extended to salespeople when buying an item; Love Hot Buttons genuinely want the sales rep to be happy too! So listen carefully. When you hear the phrase "I love this" in casual conversation, you are probably looking at an ally. Listen to what features they love and make sure the final product includes those things. Love Hot Buttons will do the rest because they are hard-wired to make the arguments that will get everyone what they need. I am convinced that's why there are so many Love Hot Buttons working in sales. They look for solutions, get excited about the possibilities and generally get consensus among the group.

Unlike Family Hot Buttons who will always pick the happiness of the children or their spouse, Love Hot Buttons unintentionally keep their children waiting to help others or leave the office very late to make sure everyone gets what they need. Greater good trumps money, relationships, and praise.

I once explained to a coworker that he was a Love Hot Button. He was really pleased with that description of himself. After some thought, he asked "So what's the down side?" I explained that it is quite common for a Love personality to become a martyr. Love Hot Buttons want so badly for others to be happy that they will exhaust themselves to achieve this goal. I didn't have the heart to tell him that weight issues are also common for this group. Taking care of everyone else gives them an excuse to avoid working out, and meals reinforce the great feelings of communion with those they love.

Wants: *Everyone to be happy.*

Avoid: *Confrontation. You will catch more flies with honey than vinegar.*

RECREATION

Do you know anyone who hops from one adventure to another? The most obvious Recreation Hot Buttons proudly display travel photos in their offices, sport bumper stickers revealing hobbies and spend much of their spare time on a boat, plane, skis, or a surf board. They pull up in SUVs complete with boat hitch and ski rack and inform you they only have a few minutes because the football game is starting.

Like the example in the intro, sometimes it is as simple as asking prospects what they do in their spare time. Most people respond with simple answers about hobbies, but someone who sees life through a Recreation filter has a different intensity in their response. These activities are more than hobbies; they define the person. It is typical for them to beam: "I'm a golfer." vs. "I like to golf." Or "I paint; watercolor mainly but I explore other mediums…"

Besides the intensity, the reaction of the people around them speaks volumes. With each Hot Button, you need to understand what is sacrificed to truly understand the person. In Recreation Hot Buttons, the most common sacrifice is family time. Consider, for example, the husband who loves sports (Football, NASCAR, Baseball, etc. . .) and starts enthusiastically describing the last event he attended. His wife wanders to a marketing display while he continues without pause. Why? This is not the first time he has forgotten their mission – he has missed other family events in order to enjoy his passions.

But not all Recreation Hot Buttons are immersed without family consideration. Some have passed it on to their children (like all good Red Sox fans) or married like-minded souls who share the enthusiasm. They are the family members who add details to dad's story and punctuate the discussions with "cool, fun, awesome".

In home building, an enormous amount of discussion and research goes into community planning. The most common notion is that people buy in communities based on proximity to jobs. This concept rings true for most of the Hot Buttons because being close to work frees up resources. However, a Recreation Hot Button thinks differently. They choose location based on the proximity to their hobby (thus golf & lake communities). They prefer to live in a community that offers plenty of room for "toys" like RVs, motorcycles, and boats.

The epitome of a recreation community is nestled in Northern California. Miles from any employment center, this recreation haven is actually built around a runway! The community streets connect to a local airport so the home owners can literally coast out of the garage in their private plane, taxi down the street and takeoff into the air. The first time I saw this community I wondered if the lure might be the prestige of the area (living in a unique neighborhood of pilots would give a lot to brag about). I quickly discarded that theory when I learned the zip code is one of the less desirable in the area. Then I walked through the neighborhood on a summer night. I observed ping pong tables in the driveways, camping gear packed into SUVs, every imaginable toy stored in the garages and, as it turns out, a lake and walking paths adjoining the community in the back. I discovered a recreation paradise! These Recreation Hot Buttons were willing to commute farther to work, give up better public schools (when they could clearly afford better districts) and live in a relatively remote area to enjoy a lifestyle that included lots of fun time!

Another tell-tale sign of a Recreation Hot Button is the lack of concern about career momentum (unless they are among the lucky few who work in the same field as their passion). "Work/Life balance" is their creed. They aren't concerned about moving up or making a ton of money. As long as their income covers the lift fees, gas for the boat, or other related expenses, they are fine. Their income is strictly needed to fund the next adventure!

There are exceptions to the casual employee and there is hidden opportunity here. The most productive, enjoyable time of my career was spent working with a brilliant Recreation Hot Button, Lori Love. By handing creative license over and challenging her to keep our training programs fun, we unleashed the best in her and everyone around us. Training materials she created were better received, awkward group situations were diffused, and the atmosphere was lively and stimulating.

SUMMARY:

Wants: *Every interaction to be fun.*

Avoid: *Bogging them down with serious subjects or details.*

SECURITY & PRIVACY

Security: the assurance that something of value will not be taken away

Privacy: freedom from the observation, intrusion, or attention of others

Most people want to be safe, right? Absolutely. But there is a group of people who use safety as the basis of all decisions. And it's not just physical safety; these individuals are concerned about the security of their property, family and their heart. This is similar to Privacy in that they don't like to reveal personal information. So how can you tell if a person is Security or a Privacy Hot Button?

One story completely sums it up. Cynthia Askew, an agent working for a top ten builder, had a visitor to her model home complex.

She had a difficult time pulling information out of him. Already engaged in our quest for Hot Button knowledge, she quickly identified signs of a Privacy Hot Button. After additional painstaking questioning, she narrowed down the features needed and got agreement from him to visit the "perfect" home. She had picked a corner lot at the end of the community where none of the other listed homes would encroach on his space. The perfect Privacy home! Well, he took one look and freaked out – he wouldn't even go in. She was confused, but stayed quiet and drove around the community for a minute.

"Stop" He said; looking at a home sandwiched into the community.

"What do you like about this home?" she asked as they unlocked the door. "The streetlight in front." he answered.

Have you guessed the Hot Button?

He is a Security Hot Button! She got it, and soon had him comfortable enough to share his personal story with her. His story isn't important here. What is important is the fact that she understood him from that point and was able to sell the customer who wouldn't even give his name a few hours before.

Privacy Hot Buttons clearly want to be left alone. They aren't afraid; they just like space. Often they are very gregarious people who keep conversation light and comfortable. They have no desire to dig into the lives of others, and want to be respected in the same way.

Do you have someone you really like at work but know very little to nothing about them? Look around. If there is a lack of personal pictures in their office or workspace, strike up a conversation. Most likely, you will get more questions than answers. Direct questions about family or personal situations will likely be fielded with generalizations like "everyone is fine, and you?"

SUMMARY:

Security Wants: No surprises. To feel that everything is under control at all times. Take their lead – make them curious so they are the ones asking the questions and feel in charge.

Avoid with Security: Surprises, new situations.

Privacy Wants: Interaction with boundaries.

Avoid with Privacy: Intrusive questions.

SEX

"Sex" combines elements of Prestige, Ego, Recreation and other Hot Buttons. The reason "Sex Sells" is that the concepts appeal to the primary Hot Button but catches the eye of the other Hot Buttons who share similar interests. The defining difference is Sex wants "<u>all</u> of it". Whereas Recreation Hot Buttons will have fun no matter what they look like, Sex Hot Buttons behave more like Prestige - all fun must look good and create envy in those not participating.

Unfortunately, it is also the most misunderstood Hot Button because the word itself makes many uncomfortable. Trainers often omit the Sex Hot Button, change the category to "Romance" or tell salespeople to talk up the master bedroom. Watered down responses miss the mark. Miscued tactics are more likely to attract Love, Ego or Family Hot Buttons.

The Sex Hot Button is your typical beer commercial. Sex Hot Buttons spend an inordinate amount of time primping, but want the party to be instant. They want to open the bottle and be popular, successful, beautiful and rich. They want instant gratification. So give them a "package" to open TODAY. Get them excited by posting pictures on Facebook, Tweeting, and using "cool" methods to get your point across.

When I managed a group that included some self-professed Sex Hot Buttons, I had to develop games, award prizes and generally create a party atmosphere to hold their attention. It is important to note, though, that this team worked extremely hard. Just like primping to prepare for a party, training emerged as an important component. They saw it as the preparation they needed for their "professional party". It would be a nightmare for them to feel awkward in any situation.

Retailers love the Sex Hot Button. Value isn't a concern and they certainly aren't worried about tomorrow. Great advertising goes a long way with these folks because it reinforces their perspective about what life should look like. Wearing designer clothes and driving expensive cars is par for the course.

Sex Hot Buttons are also conditioned to love the brevity of a commercial, so don't overcomplicate communication. If you must explain risk, find an alternate way, like sending something home with them. And definitely don't tell them there is a "process" for anything. Keeping these folks excited and in party mode is the greatest challenge. Boredom forces Sex Hot Buttons to look elsewhere for a rush, so don't give them a chance to flee.

Salespeople keep inventory – Sex Hot Buttons have no patience for ordering products. In real estate this means 30 day closings (with lots of communication and pictures). Keeping this group nailed down is challenging because there is always something that looks like it might be more fun or cool!

SUMMARY:

Wants: *Everything NOW. Keep it fun!*

Avoid: *Justifying, too much information.*

PRACTICAL APPLICATION

SALES

Although the study that identified Hot Buttons was approached with the intent to understand the buying process, my book is about communication. Having said this, it would be hard to ignore the sales application. Communication is such an integral skill for any sale.

Sales should not be about trickery or "winning". Properly executed, sales should be the natural result of meeting another's needs. Using Hot Button concepts to understand others will naturally result in more sales of any product.

Imagine how Hot Button concepts might change a car purchase. I hate the process of buying a car. I anticipate the overanxious, mostly obnoxious salesperson assaulting me with meaningless information. Now imagine that the sales rep had a way to actually connect with customers and meet true needs. There is - - using the information in this book! Hot Button dynamics could really enhance the outcome, right? We will revisit the dealership experience later in this chapter and give examples of the connections that would be improved. But suffice it to say that any salesperson can improve results by tuning into Hot Buttons.

Rather than feature dumping or rattling off stiff memorized closes, follow this system. First, identify which Hot Buttons benefit from the offered product. Using the worksheets at the back of this book, list the features of your product and WHY each Hot Button should want it. Next, LISTEN. Prospects will offer plenty of clues about their motivations. Frame the presentation in the context of THEIR perspective.

Every interaction is an opportunity for a scavenger hunt. Once you identify who your buyers really are, you will know WHY they should purchase your product. Make sure you are then prepared to sell the features in a way that matters to THE CUSTOMER.

Do you think this sounds too simple? I know the process is more complicated than that – but not by much. Handling objections that surface will be easier too. Objections are typically one of two issues; and both can be solved by knowing the prospect's Hot Button.

The first issue may signal that you haven't given enough information. Even if you've been talking for an hour, an objection may indicate that you are not discussing the *right* information. Planned presentations often include features and benefits that don't emotionally connect the potential buyer. Don't get me wrong, planned presentations and scripting definitely have their place in the sales process – as a platform to find what's important – not as a system of selling. Objections are the buyers' way of telling you that those are *your* reasons, not theirs.

I recently shopped a real estate agent who exemplifies this. Her "presentation" was close to flawless; she reviewed essential aspects of the community, home and builder story. In an hour and a half, she covered a tremendous volume of information, but failed to get me emotionally attached to the home. It was a "shotgun" approach designed to hit visitors with varied appealing pieces. The company's charitable giving, service record, and a myriad of other features were, indeed, appealing. But her presentation would have had so much more power if she had tailored that same information, and framed it to cover the objections conjured through my Hot Button lens.

For instance, while touring a beautiful, private guest suite, she discussed the views and placement of furniture but I am a Love Hot Button. What I wanted to hear was that this room would be a perfect space to comfortably accommodate my grown daughters when they spend time with us. Or that my out of town visitors would have private space to make visiting more enjoyable for everyone. The thought of a happy home would be enough to help me overcome some of the other, smaller issues with the floorplan.

The other type of objection would be a result of not reaching a Hot Button at all. Unlike the scattered shotgun approach, this typically results from a targeted pitch that misses the mark. There is only one way to avoid this pitfall –ASK QUESTIONS!

The other sales issue salespeople invariably wrestle is a lack of urgency. Wouldn't it be great if everyone bought on our time line? It's never going to be that easy BUT it can be *easier*... If you have identified a prospect's Hot Button, you will also know where the true pain resides. Urgency closes like "last one" or "priced to sell" only work if the buyer has already decided to buy; it will help them justify purchasing today. To create the urgency, their psychological need to have the product must be magnified. A good salesperson makes sure that their product meets prospects' needs. A great salesperson makes the buyer feel incomplete without it.

Going back to the auto industry, every vehicle serves the same basic need – transportation. How do you make that need urgent if the shopper already has a vehicle? The new car must meet a need that the old doesn't. For instance:

- Family – Does the old car fit everyone? Are they as safe and comfortable as they can be?

- Security – The new technology is probably going to keep everyone safer than any older model.

- Convenience – New = low maintenance = no unexpected days off for repairs. New cars are also engineered to make everything more convenient for the driver

- Finance – For a payment that is close to the current one, you can avoid the unexpected expenses of an older car.

- Love – Does the current vehicle fit everyone? Friends included? Is there room for luggage, sports equipment or delivering gifts and helping with moves?

Planting the RIGHT seed increases the discomfort with their current situation and increases the desire for a new solution. This is only possible if attention is given to the BUYERS motivations.

A group particularly immune to traditional urgency sales tactics is the Baby Boomers (and older). An exceptional sales agent once told me, "You can't convince us that a loss like this (sales) is painful. We've lost spouses, kids, businesses, fortunes and everything else. We have lived enough to know the loss of something this small will be easy". She was so right and it was a huge light bulb moment for me. (Thank you, Regina.) It underscored the importance of understanding the person vs. pushing a product. If you understand WHY a prospect walks through the door, you won't need to resort to silly "limited time offers" to make a sale.

MARKETING

If people are hard to read, advertisements aren't. A fun way to "exercise" your Hot Button muscles is to identify who is targeted in a marketing campaign. Typically, companies fall in love with their own product and make assumptions about consumers' priorities based on their own excitement. But are they hitting our true motivations or just skimming the surface?

For instance, advertisements for baby products are almost always geared to the doting mother, right? One trip to a baby store will reveal that the shoppers are more diverse than those ads would imply. I am not suggesting that this is the wrong approach; I *am* suggesting that they may be able to save money with less advertising *and* broaden their market if they appealed to others. Speaking to Security, Finance, Convenience and Prestige (for example) would give them meaningful messages that could propel more consumers to action. Take car seats; there are dozens to choose from. Here are a few examples of how they could be marketed:

- o Prestige – A brand like Britax could use their "international" safety rating to separate itself from the pack and give a reason to brag. (Security would also pay the premium for this brand based on that claim)

- o Finance – Focusing on the fact that even the least expensive seats meet federal safety standards yet save money for all of the other baby necessities

- o Convenience – Gone are the hours of adjusting straps and guessing at installation. Quick-release will save time and energy.

- o Recreation – Features like additional bases should be marketed as an easy solution for active families who want to hit the road with minimal hassle.

It is important to note that the packaging for these products does contain this information – if you know what you are looking for. The point of this exercise is to point out that these emotional buying motives are largely ignored so the buyers are forced to read the features and come to their own conclusions.

The automobile industry has improved in this regard. Most, if not all, automakers have their own "Strategic Marketing" groups that profile the buyer and shape marketing efforts. The ads cover Hot Buttons that would be most impressed by their product. Taking the best features and framing them to meet the needs of these twelve motivators can make the difference between a cool campaign that looks good and an effective campaign that sells!

One of the builders I worked for put this concept to the test. We struggled to drive traffic to a community in a fairly remote area. We invited the marketing company in and posted the Hot Buttons around the room. From there, we brainstormed about what aspects of the community would appeal to each Hot Button. We showcased our parks (Recreation/ Family), the home sizes (Prestige), the prices (Finance/Investment), and made the remote location a feature to brag about (Privacy/ Love). The campaign attracted the people who would be most likely to buy when they came in and clearly weeded out those who would be disappointed (Convenience/Sex). Without changing our product or pricing, strategic Hot Button marketing turned our community into the hottest selling community in the area.

In home building, unfortunately, this scenario is the exception. Most builder ads focus on pricing and home features. But they are not the only ones with limited focus. So many companies focus on what they think is their greatest feature and hope that the buyer will be attracted enough to make an inquiry. The best ads target multiple Hot Buttons, engaging the heart as well as the head. This targeted approach attracts the prospects by laying the groundwork for a satisfied buyer.

INTERNET MARKETING

Consumers use the shield of the internet to avoid "being sold" and to narrow down choices. Imagine the power of being able to connect with buyers and move them to action in greater numbers. An internet representative trained in Hot Buttons understands that every word is a clue revealing the final decision and uses the prospects own words to move the sale along.

I emphasize again that it is the WHY that literally opens doors. The internet prospect weighs on-line options as an apple to apple comparison. The internet search is mostly devoid of emotion. Specifications and pricing are typical search criteria *unless* someone intervenes and draws out the emotional reasons behind the purchase. Product descriptions and pictures carefully crafted to appeal to the broadest number of Hot Buttons are far superior to the current broad strokes most commonly found. But the written word will never replace a live person who asks the question "Why?". With the answer to that question, an internet representative can add emotion to the product and direct attention to the features that will most likely be appealing.

An example from the builder perspective is the following conversation:

Prospect: How much counter space is there?

Internet Rep: Did you have something specific in mind (why?)

Prospect: We do a lot of entertaining.

Internet Rep: Sounds fun, is it family? work? This plan has lots of possibilities.

Prospect: Work & friends. We are known for our parties.

Internet Rep: Now that really sounds fun! All of the homes at this community have a lot of space, but this one has space for buffet style food service on the island and still has plenty of space for drinks, etc. . . . Did you see the foyer in this one? GREAT Entry – I think we have a picture – it's a real WOW house.

(Did you figure out the Hot Button?)

The internet rep got to the point where the Prestige clues were given, so she threw in the bonus info of the foyer. Now they are picturing the party and how envious the guests will be!

The concept of internet sales is changing business, but it will not change our human nature. Making sure internet marketing venues, both written and "chats", speak to these human needs will make the most of cyber-visits.

CUSTOMER SERVICE

Great customer service isn't simply about fixing issues. It's about understanding how to make the customer happy. You have undoubtedly seen all types of businesses struggle with service. Think about how your bad experiences could have been improved. My guess is your story centers around a lack of communication. If that is the case, it stands to reason that listening with the intent to understand would create superior results.

While working at a Fortune 200 company, Rich Askew and I developed a customer service training program that focused on recognizing Hot Buttons and responding to customer needs accordingly. The program was tremendously successful. In the year we implemented training, we achieved the second highest JD Power score in the nation for our category and the highest for any division of the company. Surely our processes and products had a lot to do with our success, but we had not made any significant product changes that would account for the increase. In fact, some would argue that the scores increased *despite* changes that could have tanked us. For example, we reduced choices, changed standard features, and in some cases eliminated the traditional bells and whistles the consumer had come to expect.

We implemented the system by first educating the field teams about the importance of listening and clarifying <u>why</u> the question was being asked. For instance, some customers make it clear that they need to be present for service work. Most assume it is a trust issue but in reality the concern could be a number of things:

- Family – Wants to be sure the daily harmony is not affected by maintenance.

- Investment – Wants to make sure the repairs will withstand long term use.

- Security – Needs to know nothing is taken and would never give a key to someone else.

- Convenience – Wants to ensure the repair meets expectation so no additional effort will need to be expended.

- Finance – Can't afford anything to go wrong after warranty period, so is very concerned that all repairs are perfect.

Knowing the psychological make-up of Hot Buttons provided the Customer Relations team (and rest of the field team) an advantage over the competition. They openly discussed the Hot Buttons at team meetings and made sure all aspects of the process were tailored to suit. Security and Love Hot Buttons got more calls & emails, and Investment Hot Buttons got an abundance of information on the products used and selling features. Every experience was personalized with very little effort. Rather than dumping tons of information and lavishing additional attention on every buyer, the teams expended the same energy but just made sure efforts were well placed.

Let me be clear. Hot Button training wasn't the only reason for our success. The customer focus was the key. Hot Buttons gave us a common language and forced proactive communication. Even for those team members who didn't grasp the specific concepts, they understood the message.

WORKING WITH GROUPS

Group dynamics can be perilous to team given a mixture of personalities. It is uncommon to find a group that is comprised of the same Hot Button but it does happen. Regardless, Hot Button strategy can improve group communication and lead to cohesive, successful performance.

Certain professions attract or empower specific Hot Buttons. For instance, professors are more likely to have Ego Hot Buttons. It is a profession with a lot of autonomy; it affords them the expression of their opinions without the potential of parental dissent. Universities also encourage individual development and accomplishment by way of advanced degrees and published works.

Most attorneys I have met exemplify Prestige Hot Buttons. The title, formality of the profession, and the admiration it inspires would be attractive to someone who is very motivated by external forces. The income also allows them to live in a manner that would be the object of envy for many. By contrast, social workers, non-profit, and less lucrative careers often attract Love Hot Button professionals who want to see everyone happy.

In these cases, communicating to the primary Hot Button will likely be sufficient to keep everyone happy and productive. But what happens when the crowd is more diverse?

In group situations, the first step is to identify the areas in which each Hot Button will excel. For example, if there is an opportunity to have a leader, the Family, Prestige & Love Hot Buttons work hard to create teamwork and harmony. Recreation Hot Buttons will offer comic relief and creativity; Ego and Security folks are typically great at research and individual projects. Marrying the personalities to the tasks creates opportunities for everyone to excel, and you will maximize the efficiency and minimize drama.

Next, identify the Hot Buttons of individual group members. If the team is new to you many of the clues will be offered in their introductions: "I am a mother of 3" (family), "I sail regattas" (recreation), or short specific but unrevealing answers (privacy). As with my examples, listening and creating opportunities to observe your team will help narrow down personalities and move the team forward with a basis for purposeful and clear communication. The prior pages give you the clues needed to identify motivators. Openly identifying traits with team participation heightens group cohesiveness and understanding.

It is important to remember in public forums like meetings, that Privacy and Security Hot Buttons are not public speakers. Sex Hot Buttons lose interest unless topics are fresh and fast moving. Participation helps them stay on task. These insights may help you plan meetings and encourage participation from the people most likely to benefit. And if you are looking for someone to really bring the group out – ask the Recreation team member – Recreation Hot Buttons will help you plan fun meetings and present information in a completely fresh new way!

During one recent meeting where we identified Hot Buttons for the attendees, the team members candidly discussed how their Hot Button perspectives were affecting the team dynamic. With the heightened awareness came a conscious effort to make co-workers feel more welcome in the group as well as offering validation to the Security and Love Hot Buttons who craved acceptance. Just understanding the needs of the group was enough to make an instant improvement in the environment.

"WHO'S THE BOSS?"

I am frequently asked "Who makes the best leaders?" A great deal of successful leadership depends on individuals. Education, mentoring and experience have a huge impact on professional performance. Yet there are some characteristics that propel certain people forward – or hold them back.

> **Investment** – Invests in mentoring and other long term goals but typically doesn't work fast enough in crisis or to take advantage of situations. Plays it too safe.

> **Recreation & Family** - Doesn't want to give the time necessary to propel a business forward. If the business is on "auto-pilot" they may be able to lead effectively.

Love - Sensitivity to those around them helps them to rally teams but it also makes decisions difficult. They don't want anyone to be unhappy, so may make decisions that are great for the team, but bad for the balance sheet.

Ego – These leaders often make it to the top with their confidence and ability to sell themselves. But, the inability to listen to those around them causes issues with team morale and performance. Unless this leader is a genius in all areas (and they will think they are), business will falter. The Ego leader will run right over talent around them and make decisions based on conjecture and opinions.

Security & Privacy – These leaders will struggle with the same issues. The ability to share information and connect with groups is essential, and they just won't be comfortable doing this.

Sex – Quick fixes and quick decisions without input or research will be this leader's downfall.

Culture – Jury is out on this group because backgrounds and core beliefs can vary so greatly. Weighing heavily against them is a belief that their culture "has the answers" making them less likely to surround themselves with a healthy variety of thought and experience.

Convenience – This impatient group may be great at specific tasks, but lacks the patience to lead a large team.

Finance – Leaders need to think long term and this perspective is very short sighted.

Prestige – In my experience and observations, this group has the best likelihood of leadership success. Their concern about how others see them makes Prestige Hot Buttons ultra sensitive to data and reports that are seen in any public form like industry reports, Wall Street, etc . . . Their concern for public opinion keeps them very grounded to the organization so they know how their employees feel and see them. They want to be seen as successful, so they typically make sure the results will make them an object of envy and respect.

My observations are certainly not set in stone. Background has a lot to do with success in a management position. For instance, I know an amazing retail manager who breaks out of the mold. Inspiring, focused and extremely intelligent, she is also a Security Hot Button. The difference with this person is an Ivy League education and time spent with a therapist. Her personality hasn't changed but the security drawbacks are minimized by tactics learned in both of these ways.

By now, you realize the power of knowing an individual's perspective. Its importance is magnified when a relationship is involved. Understanding what motivates or scares the people I love helps me to frame situations in ways that will make us all happy. It also helps me understand why things may not always go as I think they should.

For example, if your spouse is a Security Hot Button, it is ever so important to reassure them of your feelings. Make sure they know the financial situation is stable and keep surprises to a minimum. A Recreation spouse, on the other hand, would be bored stiff by such behavior. They want fun, fun, and fun. This all may seem simple, but relationships are complicated and we can end up at odds with people we love. Imagine having these maddening, confusing situations narrowed to twelve possible solutions. If we take the time to think about which dynamic is at work, most issues can be resolved or even better, avoided.

Time for a scavenger hunt. Spend the next few days thinking about your immediate family. Write down their names and make notes about their hobbies, language, habits and anything else that stands out. Next ask yourself "why?" Why do they do the things they do? If you don't know, ask! Making assumptions leaves too much to misinterpretation.

Take, for example, my sister's colleague. Katie's co-worker recently took up cycling with a passion. Others at work told her he was just worried about his body. That didn't make sense to her so she asked him - "So, why the new obsession with bikes?" His casual answer left her stunned. *It is the only time in my life no one can bitch at me.*" This Love Hot Button happens to be married to a high spirited wife and has a manager who makes him accountable for every second of his work day. Jumping on his bike fills him with peace and the beauty of his surroundings – the physical attributes are just a side benefit! There were other clues to his Love Hot Button – avoiding conflict, complimenting people around him, and feeling extremely sensitive to disagreements even when they didn't involve him. Cycling gives him an outlet for joy while still making his family happy (his wife loved the physical changes and his daughter started riding with him). By asking a simple question, Katie cleared up any misconceptions.

All relationships depend on listening skills, yet we typically don't know what to listen *for*! Understanding twelve categories provides a framework for solving some of the more challenging communication issues in your life. Knowing where another is coming from allows you to know where to meet them.

Make sure to include your children or young people in your life. Like adults, their perspective will fall into these categories. Look at my own children as examples. I have four amazing girls who are completely different from each other. Our toddler Nora is already looking like she might be a Security Hot Button, but time will tell. Courtney, the youngest of our adult children, is a Security Hot Button. She craves routine and support so we spend more time one-on-one with her. We can do that without drama because the other two have more independent perspectives. The oldest, Coleen, is a Love Hot Button and she is just happy to see our family happy. And Cassie, the middle is a Recreation so she doesn't care as long as there is laughter and fun!

Take a very typical teenage/parent "discussion" after our Recreation daughter stayed out too late:

Me – "I can't believe you would worry us like this." (My rant went on for too long to print . . .)

Cass – "You are overreacting! I was just hanging with my friends" (Recreation Hot Button)

Coleen – "I didn't hear Mom say you couldn't hang out. I heard that she loves you and was worried." (Love Hot Button)

Courtney – "You might have been hurt." (Security Hot Button)

All three heard my concern and responded through their filters. It was a huge moment for me. I realized that *my responses* needed to reach them on their platform and it changed our relationships. Cass continues to enjoy herself, but makes sure her Security/Love family gets texts, emails or calls to minimize our worry!

Here are some suggestions for framing curfews:

○ Love – I want you and your friends to have a great time. Please help me relax too. 11:00 works for both of us, right?

- Recreation – 11:00 gives you lots of time for fun and gives me reason to trust you for lots more nights like this!

- Security – I worry for your safety but think being home by 11:00 will get you home before anything crazy goes on.

- Sex – Always leave them wanting more! You look great and everyone will want you to stay but the best are never the "stragglers". (Also works for Prestige)

- Ego– Don't let anyone tell you what to do. 11:00 is a time that lets you set your own pace.

Growing up is tough. Targeting communication to make sure it is heard puts you on the same side as your teen.

On the other hand, the older adults in our lives have a peculiar dynamic. In my experience working with active adults, they either get more entrenched in their perspective OR life has given them opportunities to overcome natural tendencies and become more broad minded.

Regardless of age, these are ingrained perspectives that provide us with our most basic instincts. It is up to the individuals to determine how their perspective affects relationships. And now it will be up to you to decide how to handle others!

FACEBOOK

So what about Facebook? Can you identify Hot Buttons from cyber-friendships? I think you can. People may present a little differently online but I believe core messages remain the same. Here are a few observations to help you identify a few "friends":

○ Family – Post lots of kids' photos so aunts and uncles can see how beautiful they are but the "friend count" is low. They may even use an assumed name to minimize requests and limit interactions. They don't want this to take away from real family time.

○ Investment – These folks go one of two ways. Some scorn the use of Facebook because they can't understand how someone would jeopardize a job or relationship with a site that exposes private details. Others simply limit their profile and observe others.

- Security – Most rely on Facebook to stay in touch with loved ones but rarely share. These folks tend to click the "like" button but feel less comfortable putting themselves out there for all to see with pictures and posts.

- Convenience – Perceive Facebook as a simple way to get messages to everyone without calls or individual emails. One stop shop!

- Love – The term "mega-friends" describes a person who has hundreds of friends. Love profiles are updated often and they have no hesitation about weighing in on other posts. Sounds like a whole lot of love, doesn't it?

- Prestige – Although they may be quiet for weeks, their trips are well documented with specific restaurants, tourist destinations and envied activities. Friendships are tricky; it is a balance between having enough friends and making sure they are the right people.

- Ego – They crave control and the system is not set up to accommodate them. In browsing profiles, you might notice there are a few people who regularly post but never remark or "like" other posts. These are the FB Users who are potential Ego Hot Buttons. Upon closer inspection you would find few mentions of anyone other than themselves.

Other things play into an individual's on line persona. Consider, for instance, technical savvy. If users find it difficult to navigate the system, they may be hesitant about posting. This is not a science; but Facebook offers an alternate subset of motivating clues. If you are on the fence about how to communicate, examine social media to glean the additional information you need.

SUMMARY

Literally hundreds of agents have been given Hot Button information but only a fraction has managed to use it successfully. Even fewer truly master the concepts. Why? The first reason is probably the superficial nature of the training. The materials I have seen give a brief description and assume the agent will make the connections. More importantly, personally and professionally, it is easier to stay in our own comfort zone. Those who have taken the time to understand themselves and others are brave. Their bravery is rewarded; sales come more naturally and their personal lives make more sense.

I do not propose that this is the only path to happiness or success – but it is certainly one proven way to become more engaged and assure your communication is appropriate for the situation. I sincerely hope the examples and perspective I share help you reach higher and achieve greater results and happiness.

You have a lot to digest. The following pages offer worksheets to encourage you to explore the different applications in your own life. You must be willing to work at it. The amazing co-workers and family who have embraced these concepts have used them to improve all types of relationships.

WORKSHEETS

WHO IS IN YOUR LIFE?

*This is an exercise that has proven helpful in applying
these principles to your personal life.*

1. **Name:**
   a. **Hobby**
   b. **Language**
   c. **Habits**
   d. **Car**

   Their Hot Button is _____

2. **Name:**
   a. **Hobby**
   b. **Language**
   c. **Habits**
   d. **Car**

   Their Hot Button is _____

3. **Name:**
   a. **Hobby**
   b. **Language**
   c. **Habits**
   d. **Car**

   Their Hot Button is _____

   Remember to ask WHY, WHY, WHY

SO HOW DOES ASKING HELP YOU SELL?

This is an exercise that has proven helpful in applying these principles to the sales floor.

Pick 3 Hot Buttons and write them down:

1.

2.

3.

Now, take one unique feature from your product and sell it to THAT person. Be sure to use features AND language that the customer will relate to.

Are there other features that this buyer would love? What are they? Why would those be of interest?

NEW HOME COMMUNITY EXERCISE

To maximize the effect this will have on your results, get the entire community team to work on this exercise together.

This was my team's favorite exercise. They felt it focused them on the real reasons why people buy, and how to present their product. By openly discussing these perspectives, the team reinforces the important features all through the process.

Need: Variety of magazines

Large Presentation Paper

Markers

Explain: Like communities, magazines are marketed to a target audience. Others may buy it but the majority will be drawn to the magazine for a specific reason.

Activity: Each team should pick 2 magazines that represent their buyers and discuss why. Then use the markers and poster to draw representations of their selling points and Hot Buttons. One representative should present when everyone is done, but the conversation should be open with the facilitator asking lots of "why" questions.

HOT MARKETING

*It is all about the WHY. The same feature
will appeal to a variety of consumers so use
one aspect and define it 3 different ways.*

Example: Wii and other electronic games

> *Family = Kids will play together*
>
> *Prestige = Everyone has one*
>
> *Privacy = Bowl/ Dance in the privacy of your home*

1. **Feature:**
   a. **Hot Button = why HB would like it**
   b. **=**
   c. **=**

2. **Feature:**
   a. **Hot Button = why HB would like it**
   b. **=**
   c. **=**

3. **Feature:**
   a. **Hot Button = why HB would like it**
   b. **=**
   c. **=**

HOT CUSTOMER SERVICE

Recreation	*Investment*	*Love*
Ego	*Security*	*Sex*
Culture	*Convenience*	*Family*
Finance	*Prestige*	*Privacy*

Name 3 Customer Concerns:

Ex: I want to be there when you perform the work. (Privacy – so I can make sure you don't look at anything, Family – so my wife won't be inconvenienced, Finance – because I can't afford to have this done twice, Ego – because only I know how it should be done)

1.

2.

3.

Identify several Hot Buttons for each issue. Ask yourself why each Hot Button might be concerned. Use the example as a guide.

ACKNOWLEDGEMENTS

There are a lot of patient people in my life. Not only do they put up with me on a daily basis but they have indulged me while I explored this subject for the last decade.

Professionally, Tabatha Salmon deserves special appreciation because she was the first agent to really grasp the concepts and use them to propel her to a top producer no matter where she works. She has shown me just how powerful this knowledge is on the sales floor. Tabatha may have been the practical genesis but Lori Love and Shawn Blazius were the first preachers. They helped me teach the concepts to over a hundred agents and believe, as I do, that the power of understanding unlocks a lot of possibilities.

Bryon Lehl, how can I thank you for the support, creativity and Gen Y perspective? You are amazing in every way and your passion for life is an inspiration to me.

Others like Rich Askew, helped me introduce this material to the world of customer service and Launi Cooper keeps reminding me it's not just about sales. They helped open my eyes to the broader possibilities. They are both remarkable coworkers and even better friends.

Without Shirleen VonHoffman (The Queen of Sales) I would still be saying "One of these days I will write a book." She brings out the best in me and I hope someday I can return the favor.

At home I am the luckiest woman alive. My girls could easily see the lost hours but instead they see my career as an admirable part of me. (See Love Hot Button – it was these girls waiting for my return) I love you more than I can ever say.

The rest of my family, always up for an adventure, did more than tolerate this strange hobby of interviewing people, they encouraged it! Like the example of the waitress, my family gladly jumped in to figure people out. My mom and my sister Katie were the most likely cohorts and make every outing, no matter how simple, an adventure. My brother Bryan, a wealth of ideas and feedback, has been a source of inspiration since he was just a teen. And we would all be lost without the hysterical, wise advice of my Dad who has been my sounding board for everything from sales games to parenting issues!

Writing this book brought out the best in everyone around me. Ruthy Scharer and Michelle Long gave me encouragement and perspective. While Andrea Huntington deserves a special thank you to for her attention to detail while editing.

Most of all, Cyn not only lived the last ten years listening to my theories, but always believed in this book. Thank you for the hours of feedback, and support.

Like everything in life, my experiences and revelations have been enhanced by too many people to mention here. I am grateful to everyone who has helped me explore this, and so many other aspects of life.

TO LEARN MORE:

This topic is extremely deep. Hot Buttons can be explored in many different ways and applied to several disciplines. I facilitate workshops, one-on-one coaching, and segments in team or sales meetings.

For more information email me at:
mmglover22@gmail.com

or log on to:
http://hotbuttonbook.com

ABOUT THE AUTHOR

A Sales leader with 25 years in new home construction Michelle has experienced a wide variety of markets, teams, and products. Her career launched on the East Coast working with clients to design and build homes. She was recruited to Pulte Homes as a lead sales consultant and eventually, a Top Gun Mentor. Her move to California opened new opportunities at KB Home, Pulte / Del Webb, JMC and Meritage Homes.

By thinking strategically and acting tactically, Michelle earned a reputation for improving results and helping teams surpass expectations. She has a talent for identifying the issues, creating strategic plans to improve and implementing training and processes needed to get superior results. Working with custom, modular, local and national builders has given Michelle an opportunity to learn the business from many different angles. Her diverse experiences allow her to approach every situation with a unique perspective.